To: Peggy
Happy Birthday!
Feb 2005

Love,

Sandy

God's
DAILY
ANSWER

devotions to renew your soul

God's Daily Answer
Copyright ©2003 Elm Hill Books, an imprint of J. Countryman®, a division of Thomas Nelson, Inc.
Nashville, TN 37214

With the exception of Scripture quotations, The quoted ideas expressed in this book are not, in all cases, exact quotations, as some have been edited for clarity and brevity. In all cases, the author has attempted to maintain the speaker's original intent. In some cases, quoted material for this book was obtained from secondary sources, primarily print media. While every effort has been made to ensure the accuracy of these sources, the accuracy cannot be guaranteed. For additions, deletions, corrections, or clarifications in future editions of this text, please write ELM HILL BOOKS.

Scripture quotations marked KJV are taken from the *King James Version* of the Bible.

Scripture quotations marked NCV are taken from the *International Children's Bible®, New Century Version®.* Copyright © 1986, 1988, 1999 by Tommy Nelson™, a division of Thomas Nelson, Inc., Nashville, Tennessee 37214. Used by permission.

Scripture quotations marked NKJV are taken from *The Holy Bible, New King James Version.* Copyright © 1982, 1994 by Thomas Nelson, Inc. Used by permission.

Scripture quotations marked THE MESSAGE are taken from *The Message.* Copyright © by Eugene H. Peterson, 1993, 1994, 1995, 1996. Used by permission of NavPress Publishing Group.

Scripture quotations marked NRSV are taken from the *New Revised Standard Version Bible.* Copyright © 1989 by the Division of Christian Education of the Churches of Christ in the United States of America and are used by permission.

Scripture quotations marked CEV are taken from the *Contemporary English Version.* Copyright © 1995 by the American Bible Society. Used by permission.

Scripture quotations marked NASB are taken from the *New American Standard Bible®.* Copyright © 1960, 1962, 1963, 1968, 1971, 1972, 1973, 1975, 1977, 1995, 1997 by The Lockman Foundation. Used by permission.

Scripture quotations marked TLB are taken from *The Living Bible.* Copyright © 1971, 1986. Used by permission of Tyndale House Publishers, Incorporated, Wheaton, Illinois 60189. All rights reserved.

Scripture quotations marked NLT are taken from the *Holy Bible, New Living Translation.* Copyright © 1996. Used by permission of Tyndale House Publishers, Incorporated, Wheaton, Illinois 60189. All rights reserved.

Scripture quotations marked NIV are taken from the *Holy Bible, New International Version,* (North American Edition)®. Copyright © 1973, 1978, 1984 by International Bible Society. Used by permission of Zondervan Publishing House.

Scripture quotations marked AMP are taken from *The Amplified Bible, Old Testament.* Copyright © 1965, 1987 by Zondervan Corporation, Grand Rapids, Michigan. *New Testament* copyright © 1958, 1987 by the Lockman Foundation, La Habra, California. Used by permission.

Scripture quotations marked GNT are taken from *The Good News Bible, Second Edition, Today's English Version.* Copyright © 1992 by American Bible Society. Used by permission. All rights reserved.

Manuscript written by Shanna D. Gregor in conjunction with Snapdragon Editorial Group, Inc.

Cover Design by Denise Rosser
Page Layout by Bart Dawson

ISBN: 1-4041-8439-2

Printed in the United States of America

God's
DAILY
ANSWER

devotions to renew your soul

God is inscrutable—there will always be aspects of His person that we humans aren't capable of understanding. But He knows our need for answers and has responded by giving us the Scriptures, rich oral traditions, and the witness of our hearts to let us know what we can expect from Him, how He wishes to interact with us, and the various aspects of His character. He encourages us to ask and seek, and when we do, He assures us that we will find.

If you have questions, *God's Daily Answer* was designed for you. As you read, you will hear what God has to say about issues you face in the course of your everyday life—topics like friendship, finances, work, and forgiveness. We hope you will also come to know more intimately the One who holds *all* the answers—the One who holds you in the palm of His hand.

TABLE OF CONTENTS

UNDERSTANDING IS THE REWARD OF FAITH.
Therefore, seek not to understand that you may
believe, but believe that you may understand.

SAINT AUGUSTINE OF HIPPO

FORGIVENESS

Forgive anyone who does you wrong,
just as Christ has forgiven you.

COLOSSIANS 3:13 CEV

A re you reluctant to forgive someone who has hurt or offended you, because it seems like you would be letting that person off the hook? In truth, the only person you would be letting off the hook is you!

Anger, bitterness, and resentment—the natural by-products of unforgiveness—can tie you up in knots. Give them free reign, and you'll soon find that you've done nothing to alleviate the pain you feel and everything to magnify it.

God loves you. That's why He urges you to forgive the offenses that come your way. Let them go. Distance yourself from them. In that way, you strip them of their power to do additional harm and you place yourself squarely in the path of healing.

To forgive is to set a prisoner free
and discover the prisoner was you.

AUTHOR UNKNOWN

Forgiveness is not an occasional art;
it is a permanent attitude.

MARTIN LUTHER KING JR.

When you forgive, you in no way change
the past—but you sure do change the future.

BERNARD MELTZER

Forgiveness is the key that unlocks the door
of resentment and the handcuffs of hate.
It is a power that breaks the chains of bitterness
and the shackles of selfishness.

CORRIE TEN BOOM

*Jesus said, "If you forgive others for
the wrongs they do to you, your Father
in heaven will forgive you."*

MATTHEW 6:14 CEV

CONFIDENCE

The Lord will be your confidence,
and will keep your foot from being caught.

PROVERBS 3:26 NKJV

Wouldn't it be a tragedy if you failed to reach your full potential in life or never realized your dreams and desires—simply because you lacked confidence? Yes, it would! Especially since God says it's possible to have all the confidence you need.

The secret is to know who you are—God's precious and unique child. He created you in His own image; therefore, you are of great personal worth. He promises to be with you always—guiding you, watching over you, making His resources available to you. With His help, you can overcome any obstacle that stands in your path.

God has empowered you to fulfill your destiny. Put your trust in Him, and walk confidently into the future.

Nothing can be done without
hope and confidence.

HELEN KELLER

The greater and more persistent your confidence
in God, the more abundantly you will receive
all that you ask.

ALBERT THE GREAT

There's one blessing only, the source
and cornerstone of beatitude—
confidence in self.

SENECA

Above all things, never think that
you're not good enough yourself.
My belief is that in life people will take
you at your own reckoning.

ANTHONY TROLLOPE

*You have been my hope, O Sovereign Lord,
my confidence since my youth.*

PSALM 71:5 NIV

PERSEVERANCE

Let us run the race that is before us and never give up.
HEBREWS 12:1 NCV

Perseverance—the power to stick with something until it is completed—is the key to achieving your goals and reaching your dreams. No matter how much talent, skill, intelligence, or personal charisma you have, you won't get where you want to go unless you're determined to keep your eyes focused squarely on the finish line.

Persevering means refusing to become distracted by bumps in the road—discouraging circumstances. It means discarding the negative opinions and comments of others.

God created you for a purpose, and He wants to see you succeed. When you call on Him, He promises to renew your strength. He was there at the beginning of your race, and He'll be there at the end—so persevere!

There must be a beginning to any great matter,
but the continuing to the end until
it be thoroughly finished yields the true glory.
THOMAS CARLYLE

Permanence, perseverance, and persistence
in spite of all obstacles, discouragements,
and impossibilities: It is this, that in all things
distinguishes the strong soul from the weak.

SIR FRANCIS DRAKE

Energy and persistence conquer all things.

BENJAMIN FRANKLIN

Great works are performed, not by strength,
but by perseverance.

SAMUEL JOHNSON

*You must hold on, so you can do what God wants
and receive what he has promised.*

HEBREWS 10:36 NCV

COMMITMENT

Lord, who may dwell in your sanctuary?
Who may live on your holy hill?
He ... who keeps his oath even when it hurts.

PSALM 15:1, 4 NIV

Keeping your commitments means doing what you say you're going to do—not *some* of the time, but *all* of the time. That's isn't always easy with busy schedules and changing circumstances. But if you want the respect and trust of others, it's imperative.

The best approach is to make commitments only after carefully considering whether you will be able to fulfill them. Too often, commitments are made quickly, in the heat of the moment, leaving you to discover too late they are simply impossible to keep.

Let God be your example when it comes to commitments—He always keeps His. He puts the resources of heaven and Earth behind every commitment He's made to you in the Scriptures.

He who lightly assents will seldom keep his word.

CHINESE PROVERB

Unless commitment is made, there are only
promises and hope ... but no plans.

PETER DRUCKER

If you deny yourself commitment,
what can you do with your life?

HARVEY FIERSTEIN

The moment one definitely commits oneself,
the Providence moves too. All sorts of things
occur to help that would never
otherwise have occurred.

W. H. MURRAY

As for me, I will walk in my integrity.

PSALM 26:11 NIV

EXPECTANCY

God began doing a good work in you.
And he will continue it until it is finished
when Jesus Christ comes again.

PHILIPPIANS 1:6 NCV

Imagine waiting with great expectation to see the newest canvas of a world-renowned painter. Your eyes are prepared to behold greatness. This is how you should think of yourself. After all, you were crafted by the Master Artist—God Himself. What greatness will the eyes of others see when the canvas of your life is complete?

Maybe your life, your gifts, your personality, your looks, your resources seem ordinary and commonplace to you. But commit them to God, and you will soon find they are exploding with promise and opportunity. Enhanced by the fingertips of God, the final result is certain to be extraordinary, special, unique—a true masterpiece. Expect it and you won't be disappointed.

We block Christ's advance in our lives
by failure of expectation.

WILLIAM TEMPLE

There is something new every day
if you look for it.

HANNAH HURNARD

High expectations are the key to everything.

SAM WALTON

The quality of our expectations determines
the quality of our action.

ANDRÉ GODIN

In the morning, O Lord, you hear my voice;
in the morning, I lay my requests before you
and wait in expectation.

PSALM 5:3 NIV

IDENTITY

Be imitators of God as dear children.

Ephesians 5:1 nkjv

Have you ever been introduced to someone in a way that indicated your relationship to someone else? Maybe you were identified as "Bob's secretary," "Susan's friend," "Daniel's mom." Such descriptions seldom provide a picture of the real you.

But there is one such identification you might be pleased to have others make. That is your status as a child of God. Can you imagine someone introducing you by saying, "She's full of love and peace—just like her Father God" or "He's artistic—just like his heavenly Father."

Let your relationship with God provide a great part of your personal identity. What more wonderful identity could there be than being His child?

The way in which we think of ourselves
has everything to do with how our world sees us.

Arlene Raven

Is it a small thing in your eyes to be loved
by God—to be the son, the spouse, the love,
the delight of the King of glory?

RICHARD BAXTER

He who counts the stars and calls them
by their names, is in no danger of
forgetting His own children.

CHARLES HADDON SPURGEON

Everything is good when it leaves
the Creator's hands.

JEAN-JACQUES ROUSSEAU

*Put on the new man, which was created according
to God in true righteousness and holiness.*

EPHESIANS 4:24 NKJV

TRUST

Trust in Him at all times, O people;
pour out your heart before him;
God is a refuge for us.

PSALM 62:8 NRSV

In these treacherous times, it's difficult to know whom you can trust. But there is someone you can trust unequivocally—God. People will fail you, but He never will. He is completely worthy of your trust.

God does not promise you will never encounter difficult situations or painful circumstances. But He does promise they will never be more than the two of you, together, can manage. He also promises good will come from any and every situation that touches your life—even heartache and tragedy. And most wonderful of all—He says that nothing will be able to separate you from His love.

Place your trust in God. He always keeps His promises.

I have held many things in my hands,
and I have lost them all; but whatever I have
placed in God's hands, that I still possess.

CORRIE TEN BOOM

Trust in God and you are never to be
confounded in time or in eternity.

DWIGHT MOODY

All I have seen teaches me to trust
the Creator for all I have not seen.

RALPH WALDO EMERSON

Trust the past to God's mercy,
the present to God's love
and the future to God's providence.

SAINT AUGUSTINE OF HIPPO

Trust in the Lord with all your heart,
and do not rely on your own insight.

PROVERBS 3:5 NRSV

GOD'S FORGIVENESS

*If we confess our sins, He is faithful and just
to forgive us our sins and to cleanse us
from all unrighteousness.*

1 JOHN 1:9 NKJV

You may find it difficult to forget your mistakes, your missteps, your sins. But God doesn't—He forgives *and* forgets. Imagine a piece of paper filled with confessions of your past indiscretions. Suppose every single sin you ever committed appears on that page. Like a child might hand a paper with a bad grade to his or her parent, you reluctantly give the list of your sins to God.

God takes that paper and crumples it into a tiny ball. Then He throws it into a burning fire—it is consumed—never to be remembered again.

God's forgiveness is just like that. Once He has forgiven you, He will never bring it up again—so why would you? Go on your way and sin no more!

There is only one person God cannot forgive:
the one who refuses to come to
him for forgiveness.

AUTHOR UNKNOWN

Forgiveness does not mean the cancellation of all consequences of wrongdoing. It means the refusal on God's part to let our guilty past affect His relationship with us.

AUTHOR UNKNOWN

I think that if God forgives us, we must forgive ourselves.

C. S. LEWIS

The most marvelous ingredient in the forgiveness of God is that he also forgets, the one thing a human being can never do.

OSWALD CHAMBERS

You, Lord, are good, and ready to forgive.

PSALM 86:5 NKJV

FRESH START

You have begun to live the new life.
In your new life, you are being made new.
You are becoming like the One who made you.

COLOSSIANS 3:10 NCV

In the midst of life's challenges, God gives you a wonderful gift—a fresh start. No matter what choices you have made in the past, turning over your mistakes to God will put you on the path to a bright future.

Think about it this way: a house shows signs of past abuse, neglect, and turbulent weather. The painter comes along and strips off the old peeling paint, sands the boards, and applies a fresh, clean coat of paint. Signs of the past are gone for good, and the house has a fresh new start.

Likewise, God has given you the honor and privilege of being able to shake off past mistakes and experience a fresh start. He is the God of new beginnings.

If you have made mistakes, even serious ones,
there is always another chance for you.
What we call failure is not the falling down,
but the staying down.

MARY PICKFORD

I like sunrises, Mondays, and new seasons.
God seems to be saying,
"With me you can always start afresh."

ADA LUM

With each sunrise, we start anew.

AUTHOR UNKNOWN

Each day is a new life. Seize it. Live it.

DAVID GUY POWERS

If anyone is in Christ, there is a new creation:
everything old has passed away;
see, everything has become new!

2 CORINTHIANS 5:17 NRSV

WORK

The plans of the diligent lead surely to plenty.

PROVERBS 21:5 NKJV

God created the entire universe in six days, and as each part was completed, He looked it over and said, "It is good." He undertook His work with diligence and was rewarded with a sense of satisfaction.

God wants you to gain satisfaction in return for your diligence as well—and you can. No matter what task lies before you, you have the power to transform it from being an exhausting struggle to a creative joy, simply by changing the way you view it.

Take a second look at the task at hand—reconciling your checkbook, changing diapers, or traveling on a long flight to a business meeting. Ask God to open your eyes to the creative energy in that task. Then go about it with your whole heart. You'll enjoy your work a whole lot more, and God will bless you for it.

God is the Best and Most Orderly Workman of all.

COPERNICUS

There's no labor a man can do that's undignified,
if he does it right.

BILL COSBY

Honest labor bears a lovely face.

THOMAS DEKKER

He who labors diligently need never despair,
for all things are accomplished
by diligence and labor.

MENANDER

Whatever your task, put yourselves into it,
as done for the Lord and not for your masters.

COLOSSIANS 3:23 NRSV

CHILDREN

Children are a heritage from the Lord, the fruit of the womb a reward. As arrows are in the hand of a warrior, so are the children of one's youth.

PSALM 127:3–4 AMP

When Jesus was here on Earth, He often took time for children. He held them, blessed them, and told His disciples their tender innocence and simple faith were the essence of the Kingdom of God.

If you have children, you no doubt know that God has entrusted you with a most precious treasure. He expects you to give them your very best and raise them with an understanding of His goodness and grace.

Just as an archer aims and then shoots an arrow toward his target, God has given you the ability to direct and send forth your children. He has also given you His word that He will be there to help you every step of the way.

Children must be valued as our most priceless possession.

JAMES DOBSON

One laugh of a child will make
the holiest day more sacred still.

ROBERT GREEN INGERSOLL

There is just one way to bring up a child
in the way he should go and that is
to travel that way yourself.

ABRAHAM LINCOLN

The heart of a child is the most precious of
God's creation.

JOSEPH L. WHITTEN

Train children in the right way,
and when old, they will not stray.

PROVERBS 22:6 NRSV

MERCY

*God's mercy is so abundant, and his love for us is
so great, that while we were spiritually dead in
our disobedience he brought us to life with Christ.*

Before you ever thought about Him, a
merciful God loved you and executed a
plan to redeem your life. His goodness and mercy
defeated sin and judgment, and opened the way of
peace for you. That mercy is available to you every
day.

If you feel you have failed God, His mercy will
free you from guilt and condemnation. If you feel you
have failed someone else, His mercy will be upon you
as you seek to make things right. God's mercy will
always be available for you to pass along to others.

We all need mercy—both to give and to
receive. God is the source. Look to Him. He will
give you all you need.

Mercy is compassion in action.

Nothing graces the Christian soul
as much as mercy.

SAINT AMBROSE

He who demands mercy and shows none ruins
the bridge over which he himself is to pass.

THOMAS ADAMS

Two works of mercy set a man free:
forgive and you will be forgiven,
and give and you will receive.

SAINT AUGUSTINE OF HIPPO

*Blessed are the merciful,
for they will be shown mercy.*

MATTHEW 5:7 NIV

SPEECH

When you talk, do not say harmful things.
But say what people need—words that will
help others become stronger.

Ephesians 4:29 NCV

God's spoken words were powerful enough to create the universe. You are made in His image; therefore, your words have power too—the power to hurt or heal, encourage or condemn, safeguard the truth or foster lies.

God wants you to use your words in the same way He does—for good. It will mean a decision of your will and a lot of determination, but your words can make you a creative force for good in the world.

Ask God to help you take charge of your tongue and thus control the power of your spoken words. God's words created the universe and all it contains. Imagine the wonderful things your words can do.

Little keys can open big locks.
Simple words can express great thoughts.

William Arthur Ward

Good words are worth much, and cost little.

GEORGE HERBERT

Speaking without thinking is
shooting without aiming.

SIR WILLIAM GURNEY BENHAM

Kind words produce their image on men's souls;
and a beautiful image it is. They smooth,
and quiet, and comfort the hearer.

BLAISE PASCAL

*Choose your words carefully and be ready to give
answers to anyone who asks questions.*

COLOSSIANS 4:6 CEV

HEAVEN

Blessed be the God and Father of our Lord Jesus Christ, which according to his abundant mercy hath begotten us again unto a lively hope by the resurrection of Jesus Christ from the dead, to an inheritance incorruptible, and undefiled, and that fadeth not away, reserved in heaven for you.

1 PETER 1:3–4 KJV

Heaven is the home God has prepared for those He has redeemed through His Son, Jesus Christ. It's a real place—a place full of God's perfect love, joy, and peace. There is no pain there, no tears. So grand is it that the Bible only reveals small glimpses of its marvels.

One day you will see heaven and all its magnificence. Until then, there is only one way to experience a *taste* of heaven right here on Earth—by spending time in sweet communion with God.

Spending eternity in heaven is indeed something to look forward to. But until you can walk its streets, get into God's presence, and treat yourself to a *taste* of what your future holds.

Blessed assurance, Jesus is mine!
O what a foretaste of glory divine!

FANNY CROSBY

Earth has no sorrow that heaven cannot heal.

THOMAS V. MOORE

Heaven is a prepared place for a prepared people.

LEWIS SPERRY CHAFER

God's retirement plan is out of this world.

AUTHOR UNKNOWN

Our bodies are like tents that we live in here on earth.
But when these tents are destroyed, we know that
God will give each of us a place to live.
These homes will not be buildings that someone
has made, but they are in heaven
and will last forever.

2 CORINTHIANS 5:1 CEV

PROTECTION

God will cover you with his wings;
you will be safe in his care;
his faithfulness will protect and defend you.

PSALM 91:4 GNT

Try to remember a time as a child when you were frightened by a storm in the night. You probably called out to your parents or even crawled into bed with them. As you felt the warmth of their embrace and listened to their comforting words, you went right back to sleep—quickly forgetting the storm that continued to rage just outside the window.

God—your heavenly Father—wants to be your Comforter and Protector today. He has even commissioned His angels to guard you at all times. He has promised to never leave you alone or forsake you. As you meditate on these truths, your heart will be warmed and you will be at peace.

Commit yourself to His loving care. He's always watching over you.

Prayer is the key that shuts us up under his protection and safeguard.

JACQUES ELLUL

Security is not the absence of danger,
but the presence of God,
no matter what the danger.

AUTHOR UNKNOWN

Safe am I. Safe am I, in the hollow of His hand.

OLD SUNDAY SCHOOL SONG

Those who walk in God's shadow are
not shaken by the storm.

ANDREA GARNEY

The Lord will keep you from all evil;
he will keep your life. The Lord will keep
your going out and your coming in from
this time on and forevermore.

PSALM 121:7–8 NRSV

FAITH

Faith is the substance of things hoped for,
the evidence of things not seen.

HEBREWS 11:1 NKJV

Imagine a man or woman who wants to participate in a long bicycle trip, but hasn't ridden in years. On the first day, the person in question can only ride half a mile. But each day, the person is able to go a little further. Soon, leg muscles begin to grow strong and the individual is able to ride the bike for ten miles.

Faith can be compared to those leg muscles. It also grows strong with exercise. God has given you the ability to believe, to love, to acknowledge Him. And as you take one small step at a time in His direction, believing His Word, your faith will grow stronger and stronger. Soon, you will be achieving things you never dreamed possible.

Faith is nothing at all tangible.
It is simply believing God.

HANNAH WHITALL SMITH

The act of faith is more than a bare statement
of belief; it is a turning to the face of
the living God.

CHRISTOPHER BRYANT

Faith is to believe what you do not yet see:
the reward for this faith is to see
what you believe.

SAINT AUGUSTINE OF HIPPO

Faith tells us of things we have never seen
and cannot come to know by our natural senses.

SAINT JOHN OF THE CROSS

Jesus said, "I tell you the truth,
if you have faith as small as a mustard seed,
you can say to this mountain,
'Move from here to there' and it will move.
Nothing will be impossible for you."

MATTHEW 17:20 NIV

ACCEPTANCE

*You are a chosen race, a royal priesthood,
a dedicated nation, [God's] own purchased,
special people.*

1 PETER 2:9 AMP

The desire for acceptance is very human. We long for it, seek it, and do all we can to acquire it. With some people the need goes so deep that it colors every aspect of their lives—what they wear, how they speak, where they go, even their opinions and behaviors.

How sad these people have never discovered God loves and accepts them just as they are. Don't let that be said of you. After all, God created you. You are precious and priceless in His sight. You have *His* seal of approval.

If you are desperately seeking acceptance, look to God. Ask Him to show you what He sees in you. Once you see yourself as He sees you, your search will be over.

Accept the fact that you are accepted.

PAUL TILLICH

I f God accepts me as I am,
then I had better do the same.

HUGH MONTEFIORE

J esus accepts you the way you are,
but loves you too much to leave you that way.

LEE VENDEN

J ust as I am, thou wilt receive, will welcome,
pardon, cleanse, relieve; because thy promise
I believe, O Lamb of God, I come.

CHARLOTTE ELLIOTT

To the praise of the glory of his grace,
wherein he hath made us accepted in the beloved.

EPHESIANS 1:6 KJV

DECISIONS

*If any of you is lacking in wisdom,
ask God, who gives to all generously
and ungrudgingly, and it will be given you.*

JAMES 1:5 NRSV

Each day, you are faced with decisions that must be made—and made well, because each one will affect your life and the lives of those around you. How can you guarantee that you'll always choose wisely? You can't. You're human, and you're going to make mistakes from time to time. But there are ways to increase your odds.

First, avoid making decisions based primarily on emotion. Feelings can cloud your judgment. Second, become informed. Before you make up your mind, gather as much pertinent information as possible. Third, ask God to infuse your knowledge with His wisdom and to follow that up with His peace. When you've considered the facts and feel God's peace, your decisions are apt to be ones you can live with.

Yes and no are the two most important words that you will ever say. These are the two words that determine your destiny in life.

AUTHOR UNKNOWN

God gives man a will but he must make
the right choices.

FULTON J. SHEEN

There is a time when we must firmly choose
the course we will follow, or the relentless drift of
events will make the decision.

HERBERT V. PROCHNOW

We must make the choices that enable us
to fulfill the deepest capacity of our real serves.

THOMAS MERTON

I bless the Lord who gives me counsel;
in the night also my heart instructs me.

PSALM 16:7 NRSV

THANKFULNESS

O Lord my God, I will give you thanks forever.
PSALM 30:12 NIV

Life is full of things to be grateful for—small acts of kindness and generosity, words of hope and encouragement, gifts of love and caring. Look around you and see how many you can count in just a few moments.

Perhaps on your way to work you passed a tree full of lovely spring blossoms. Or one of your coworkers brought you a cup of coffee. Or your spouse gave you a long embrace before leaving the house. It could be you were kissed by a child, snuggled by a kitten, comforted by a touch.

A thankful heart takes time to notice those small, precious gifts. Are you thankful for the little things that come your way? Why don't you let God know.

Thou has given so much to me.
Give me one thing more—a grateful heart.

GEORGE HERBERT

Thanksgiving is good but thanks-living is better.

MATTHEW HENRY

No duty is more urgent than that of
returning thanks.

SAINT AMBROSE

Thanksgiving is the end of all human conduct,
whether observed in words or works.

J. B. LIGHTFOOT

Give thanks in all circumstances;
for this is the will of God in Christ Jesus for you.

1 THESSALONIANS 5:18 NRSV

WISDOM

*The wisdom from above is first pure, then peaceable,
gentle, willing to yield, full of mercy and good fruits,
without a trace of partiality or hypocrisy.*

JAMES 3:17 NRSV

Imagine purchasing something that has "Assembly required" on the label. Now think about getting out the tools, parts, and directions for the project, only to discover that a picture of the finished product has not been included. That's the way some situations in your life can seem. That's why you need God's wisdom to pull it all together.

God's wisdom sees the big picture and gives you perspective. It may help you see options that were not apparent before. His wisdom can help you make good choices.

Life is tricky. God wants you to go forward with everything you need for success. That includes the big picture only He can provide.

Men may acquire knowledge,
but wisdom is a gift direct from God.

BOB JONES

Wisdom is the application of knowledge.

AUTHOR UNKNOWN

Common sense suits itself to the ways of the world. Wisdom tries to conform to the ways of heaven.

JOSEPH JOUBERT

Knowledge comes, but wisdom lingers.

ALFRED LORD TENNYSON

The Lord gives wisdom; from his mouth come knowledge and understanding.

PROVERBS 2:6 NRSV

FRIENDSHIP

A man that hath friends must shew himself friendly.
PROVERBS 18:24 KJV

Do you know a person who seems to have an abundance of friends? Look closely and you'll probably notice that person reaching out, initiating toward others, cultivating new relationships.

Too often people sit around waiting for others to come to them. But friendship, like most valuable things in life, requires an investment of time and effort. If you want it, you must be willing to work for it.

If you'd like to have more friends, go out and get them. Practice those virtues that you feel a good friend would have. Be an encourager and an attentive listener. Show an interest in other people. Soon you'll be wondering how you're going to find time for all the new people in your life.

The only way to have a friend is to be a friend.
RALPH WALDO EMERSON

Many a friendship—long, loyal,
and self-sacrificing—rested at first upon
no thicker a foundation than a kind word.

FREDERICK W. FABER

You can make more friends in two months by
becoming interested in other people than
you can in two years by trying to get
other people interested in you.

DALE CARNEGIE

Getting people to like you is only
the other side of liking them.

NORMAN VINCENT PEALE

A friend loves at all times.

PROVERBS 17:17 NASB

ETERNAL LIFE

*Surely your goodness and love will be
with me all my life. And I will live in
the house of the Lord forever.*

PSALM 23:6 NCV

Eternal life isn't just living forever in heaven with God—although that's certainly part of it. Your promise for eternal life includes the here and now. If you've entrusted yourself to God's care and have received His gift of salvation, you have the reality of eternal life today. You don't have to wait to die an earthly death before you can enjoy it.

The Bible says that God's goodness and mercy will follow you all the days of your life. So why live another day without hope, without joy, without meaning. Reach out to God. Trade in your old life for a new one, and start living life to the fullest—all the days of your life here on Earth—and later in heaven.

The life of faith does not earn eternal life;
it is eternal life.

WILLIAM TEMPLE

People who dwell in God dwell in
the eternal Now.

MEISTER ECKHART

Where, except in the present,
can the Eternal be met?

C. S. LEWIS

Eternity is not something that begins after
you are dead. It is going on all the time.

CHARLOTTE PERKINS GILMAN

Whoever believes in the Son has eternal life.

JOHN 3:36 NRSV

BLESSINGS

I will send down showers in season;
there will be showers of blessing.

EZEKIEL 34:26 NIV

Y ou know what a pleasant feeling it is to indulge your children with gifts—so pleasant that you probably have to restrain yourself at times for their own good. Your heavenly Father loves to pour gifts and blessings on His children too. Look around and you'll see the wonderful things He's already placed in your life.

Notice the finger-painted sunrise God made just for you. Consider the joy, love, comfort, encouragement, and caring God has poured out on you through your friends and family members. Then close your eyes and meditate on the greatest blessing of all—that God loves you. Thank your Father for all of your many blessings. Your love and thanks bless Him in return.

God is more anxious to bestow his blessings
on us than we are to receive them.

SAINT AUGUSTINE OF HIPPO

The more we count the blessings we have,
the less we crave the luxuries we haven't.

WILLIAM ARTHUR WARD

The best things are nearest; breath in
your nostrils, light in your eyes,
flowers at your feet, duties at your hand,
the path of God just before you.

ROBERT LOUIS STEVENSON

Reflect upon your present blessings, of which
every man has many, not on your past misfortunes,
of which all men have some.

CHARLES DICKENS

The Lord bless you and keep you; the Lord make
his face to shine upon you, and be gracious to you;
the Lord lift up his countenance upon you,
and give you peace.

NUMBER 6:24–26 NRSV

CHARACTER

Let endurance have its full effect,
so that you may be mature and complete,
lacking in nothing.

JAMES 1:4 NRSV

Character is commonly defined as moral strength—the ability to consistently do the right thing for the right reasons. How do you stack up when it comes to character?

You may already be a person whose strength of character is well established. But if you aren't, you can be. No matter what you have done in the past, you have an opportunity each day to do what is right; and each time you do what is right, you plant a seed of character in your life.

Add to that one more ingredient—endurance. As you sustain a pattern of choosing to do what is right, you will be well on your way to becoming the strong person of character God has always intended you to be.

We first make our habits, then our habits make us.

JOHN DRYDEN

Character is what you are in the dark.

DWIGHT MOODY

Reputation is what men and women think of us.
Character is what God
and the angels know of us.

THOMAS PAINE

Character is not in the mind. It is in the will.

FULTON JOHN SHEEN

*The Lord guides the humble in what is right
and teaches them his way.*

PSALM 25:9 NIV

FAMILY

*God is the One who made all things. And all things
are for his glory. God wanted to have many sons share
his glory. So God made perfect the One who leads
people to salvation. He made Jesus a perfect
Savior through Jesus' suffering.*

HEBREWS 2:10 NCV

God's desire to have a family—a group of
people related to each other—is the
reason He created man. He desired the fellowship
of many sons and daughters, beginning with Adam
and Eve. When Adam and Eve fell, God's family was
in jeopardy of remaining separated from Him for
eternity.

God loves His family more than any man or
woman could love theirs. So He sent Jesus, His only
Son, to reunite Him with His family once again.
When you choose to cross the bridge created by Jesus'
death and triumphant resurrection, you become a
child of the Most High God, and join a family like
none you have ever known before.

A family is a place where principles are hammered
and honed on the anvil of everyday living.

CHARLES R. SWINDOLL

Loving relationships are a family's best
protection against the challenges of the world.

BERNIE WIEBE

The family is the most basic unit of government.
As the first community to which a person is
attached and the first authority under which
a person learns to live, the family establishes
society's most basic values.

CHARLES W. COLSON

As the family goes, so goes the nation
and so goes the whole world in which we live.

POPE JOHN PAUL II

I bow my knees before the Father, from whom every
family in heaven and on earth takes its name.

EPHESIANS 3:14–15 NRSV

FINANCES

Riches and honor come from you, and you rule over all. In your hand are power and might; and it is in your hand to make great and to give strength to all.

1 CHRONICLES 29:12 NRSV

Whether you have plenty of money or not enough, chances are you spend a lot of time thinking about it. Where should you invest your excess? Where can you come up with the difference between what you have and what you need? In both cases, God is available to help. He can bring wisdom to your efforts and help you keep financial issues in proper perspective.

Begin by recognizing God as your Source—your Provider. All you have now, and all you will ever have, come from Him.

If you have more than enough, ask God to help you be a good steward of what He has given you. If you have too little, ask Him to help you find ways to make up the difference.

If a person gets his attitude toward money straight,
it will help straighten out almost
every other area in his life.

BILLY GRAHAM

Money has never yet made anyone rich.

SENECA

There is no portion of money that is our money
and the rest God's money. It is all his;
he made it all, gives it all, and he has simply
trusted it to us for his service.

ADOLPHE MONOD

Use everything as if it belongs to God. It does.
You are his steward.

AUTHOR UNKNOWN

Keep your lives free from the love of money.
And be satisfied with what you have. God has said,
"I will never leave you; I will never forget you."

HEBREWS 13:5 NCV

JUSTICE

*All have sinned and fall short of the glory of God,
and are justified freely by his grace through
the redemption that came by Christ Jesus.*

ROMANS 3:23 NIV

A re you struggling with a situation in your life in which you feel you were unjustly treated? Have you been wondering if God knows or cares? The Bible says He does, and He will see that justice is done in your case. But remember this: God's justice is carried out in His own time and in His own way.

God's justice is tempered by His mercy and His understanding of what is best for each person in His care. He will not rush to judgment. He is patient even with those who err. The good news is that in another situation, that person may be you.

Don't allow bitterness to control your life. Commit yourself to God, and trust Him to deal justly and mercifully on your behalf.

The pearl of justice is found in the heart of mercy.

SAINT CATHERINE OF SIENA

J ustice is truth in action.

JOSEPH JOUBERT

T rue peace is not only the absence of tension;
it is the presence of justice.

MARTIN LUTHER KING JR.

N o human actions ever were intended by
the Maker of men to be guided by balances of
expediency, but by balances of justice.

JOHN RUSKIN

*The Lord God has told us what is right
and what he demands: "See that justice is done,
let mercy be your first concern,
and humbly obey your God."*

MICAH 6:8 CEV

HEALTH

The very God of peace sanctify you wholly; and I pray God your whole spirit and soul and body be preserved blameless unto the coming of our Lord Jesus Christ.

1 THESSALONIANS 5:23 KJV

God created you in His image. That means you are triune—a spirit being who lives in a body and has a mind. He wants you to experience health in every area—each part working in harmony with the others. That's the only way you can become all He has created you to be.

Your spirit can only be nourished and kept healthy as you spend time with God. A healthy mind requires a regular diet of positive thoughts and images. Try the Bible. It's filled with God's words of love and encouragement. A healthy spirit and mind provide a foundation of wisdom and understanding on which to maintain a healthy body.

Don't settle for health in only one part of your being. Ask God to help you pursue wholeness.

To be "whole" is to be spiritually, emotionally, and physically healthy.
Jesus lived in perfect wholeness.

COLIN URQUHART

The part can never be well unless
the whole is well.

PLATO

He who has health has hope,
and he who has hope has everything.

ARAB PROVERB

Our prayers should be for a sound mind in a
healthy body.

JUVENAL

*I wish above all things that thou mayest prosper
and be in health, even as thy soul prospereth.*

3 JOHN 2 KJV

MEDITATION

Let the words of my mouth and the meditation of my heart be acceptable in Your sight, O Lord, my strength and my Redeemer.

PSALM 19:14 NKJV

A quiet walk by the lake, an hour sitting near the fireplace, or just gathering your thoughts at the kitchen table are all savored times of reflection. They can also be moments alone with God, meditating on the reality of His intervention in your life.

The Bible says God walked with Adam and Eve in the Garden of Eden. They spent time together in the cool of the evening. God also wants to spend time with you. He longs for you to know Him better, to understand His wonderful plans and purposes for your life. He wants to hear what you have to say as you meditate on His goodness. Focus your meditation on God. He's always ready to meet you.

Meditation is the activity of calling to mind, and thinking over, and dwelling on, and applying to oneself, the various things that one knows about the works and ways and purposes and promises of God.

J. I. PACKER

Let us leave the surface and,
without leaving the world, plunge into God.

TEILHARD DE CHARDIN

In the rush and noise of life, as you have
intervals, step home within yourselves
and be still. Wait upon God, and feel
his good presence; this will carry you
evenly through your day's business.

WILLIAM PENN

Those who draw water from the wellspring of
meditation know that God dwells
close to their hearts.

TOYOHIKO KAGAWA

Within your temple, O God,
we meditate on your unfailing love.

PSALM 48:9 NIV

INTEGRITY

*We take thought beforehand and aim to be honest
and absolutely above suspicion, not only in
the sight of the Lord but also in the sight of men.*

2 CORINTHIANS 8:21 AMP

Integrity can be defined as uprightness of heart. It is the primary characteristic of a person who regularly and consistently does what is right. Such a person lives an honest life, honors others, and can be counted on to keep commitments. A person of integrity gives 100 percent on the job, and their spouse lives securely because he or she can be trusted.

Are you a person of integrity? Does your character set you apart from the crowd? Do you draw a line in the sand and refuse to cross it for any reason? Look at your heart for a moment. With God's help, you can live a life of integrity that is pleasing to Him.

Integrity is the first step to true greatness.

CHARLES SIMMONS

There is no such thing as
a minor lapse of integrity.

TOM PETERS

Integrity is not a conditional word. It doesn't
blow in the wind or change with the weather.
It is your inner image of yourself, and if you
look in there and see a man who won't cheat,
then you know he never will.

JOHN D. MACDONALD

Integrity has no need of rules.

ALBERT CAMUS

Let integrity and uprightness preserve me;
for I wait on thee.

PSALM 25:21 KJV

BELIEF

These [miracles] are written that you may believe that
Jesus is the Christ, the Son of God,
and that believing you may have life in His name.

JOHN 20:31 NKJV

Belief can be defined as a conviction so firm that a person accepts it as truth—even if it isn't. For that reason, it's important to examine the evidence before believing in any premise—even the existence of God.

Look around you and take in the physical evidence, a world of exquisite beauty and breathtaking detail. Add to that the testimony of others. Ask people why they believe in God, and then evaluate what they have to say. Read the Bible and see what God has to say about himself. Last of all, ask God to make himself real to you. Do all the pieces fit?

God encourages an honest search for truth. He wants you to be certain your belief in Him is well placed.

We can believe what we choose.
We are answerable for what we choose to believe.

JOHN HENRY NEWMAN

I now believe that the balance of reasoned
considerations tells heavily in favor of
the religious, even of the Christian
view of the world.

C. E. M. JOAD

If easy belief is impossible, it is that
we may learn what belief is
and in whom it is to be placed.

F. D. MAURICE

The point of having an open mind,
like having an open mouth,
is to close it on something solid.

G. K. CHESTERTON

He that cometh to God must believe that he is,
and that he is a rewarder of them
that diligently seek him.

HEBREWS 11:6 KJV

NATURE

Birds find nooks and crannies in your house,
sparrows and swallows make nests there.
They lay their eggs and raise their young,
singing their songs in the place where we worship.
God of the Angel Armies! King! God!

PSALM 84:3 THE MESSAGE

All over the earth, you can see the artistry of God. Mountains reach up toward the sky, majestically pointing toward their Creator—their snow-capped peaks offering silent praise. Farmers' fields of grain wave to the King of Kings. All the earth grows tall, as if reaching up to receive His touch. Animals of every kind show gratitude to their Maker. Birds sing, fireflies dance, and little furry creatures scurry in a fast festivity of life.

God created nature for His glory, and when you look, you can see a glimpse of His greatness. It is a reflection of an even greater glory—that of His presence in the life of a human being life you.

Nature is but a name for an effect
whose cause is God.

WILLIAM COWPER

The more I study nature,
the more I am amazed at the Creator.

LOUIS PASTEUR

I love to think of nature as an unlimited
broadcasting station through which
God speaks to us every hour,
if we will only tune in.

GEORGE WASHINGTON CARVER

We can almost smell the aroma of God's beauty
in the fresh spring flowers. His breath surrounds us
in the warm summer breezes.

GALE HEIDE

The heavens declare the glory of God;
and the firmament sheweth his handiwork.

PSALM 19:1 KJV

GOD'S FAITHFULNESS

*God is faithful; by him you were called into
the fellowship of his Son, Jesus Christ our Lord.*

1 CORINTHIANS 1:9 NRSV

It's a wonderful blessing to have a faithful friend—someone who is there to see you through good times and bad times, when it's convenient and when it isn't. A friend who never leaves your side, whose love is strong and constant, who is always ready to listen, provide wise counsel, and defend you. Do you have a friend like that? You may not know it, but you do.

God wants to be your faithful friend. And unlike earthly friends, He is armed with more than good intentions. God will never fail you. He will be by your side no matter where you are or what you are doing. Open your heart to the most faithful friend you will ever know.

Though men are false, God is faithful.

MATTHEW HENRY

What more powerful consideration can be
thought on to make us true to God,
than the faithfulness and truth of God to us?

WILLIAM GURNALL

God is faithful, and if we serve him faithfully,
he will provide for our needs.

SAINT RICHARD OF CHICHESTER

In God's faithfulness lies eternal security.

CORRIE TEN BOOM

Thy mercy, O Lord, is in the heavens;
and thy faithfulness reacheth unto the clouds.

PSALM 36:5 KJV

SCRIPTURE

*Using the Scriptures, the person who serves God
will be ready and will have everything he needs
to do every good work.*

2 TIMOTHY 3:17 NCV

The Bible is an amazing book. It is, by many accounts, the greatest collection of literature, history, prophecy, and principles for daily living ever compiled. But the Holy Scriptures can do more than teach you how to live; they can literally put you in touch with the Giver of Life.

The Bible chronicles God's intervention with the human race. It reveals His role as Creator, Redeemer, and Coming King. It describes Him as Friend, Advisor, Comforter, and Guide. It tells you everything you will ever need to know about how to enter into a relationship with Him.

If you've always wanted to know God, open your Bible and begin to read. You're sure to find Him there.

God did not write a book and send it by messenger
to be read at a distance by unaided minds.
He spoke a Book and lives in His spoken words,
constantly speaking His words and causing
the power of them to persist across the years.

A. W. TOZER

GOD'S DAILY ANSWER
devotions to renew your soul

The Bible was given to bear witness to one God,
Creator and Sustainer of the universe,
through Christ, Redeemer of sinful man.
It presents one continuous story—
that of human redemption.

M. F. UNGER

When you read God's word, you must
constantly be saying to yourself,
"It is talking to me and about me."

SØREN KIERKEGAARD

When you have read the Bible,
you will know it is the word of God,
because you will have found it the key to
your own heart, your own happiness and your duty.

WOODROW WILSON

The word of the Lord endures forever.

1 PETER 1:25 NKJV

LOVE

Beloved, let us love one another, for love is from God;
and everyone who loves is born of God
and knows God.

1 JOHN 4:7 NASB

Jesus set an example of love that surpasses any the world had ever known before He came. It was and is an inclusive love that has been poured out equally on the most godly saint and the most despicable sinner. It knows nothing of social status—turning a blind eye to wealth, fame, and fortune. It is color blind, looking past the outward appearance to the heart.

God has called you to love others in the same way He loves you. That may seem impossible, but you can do it if you are willing to open yourself as a channel, letting God's love flow through you to others.

Ask God to help you love others as He loves you. Be part of the greatest circle of love in the universe.

Love seeks one thing only:
the good of the one loved.

THOMAS MERTON

I have found the paradox that if
I love until it hurts, then there is no hurt,
but only more love.

MOTHER TERESA

Love is the thing that makes life possible or,
indeed, tolerable.

ARNOLD JOSEPH TOYNBEE

Love, like warmth, should beam forth on
every side and bend to every necessity of
our brethren.

MARTIN LUTHER

*If we love one another, God lives in us,
and his love is perfected in us.*

1 JOHN 4:12 NRSV

LIFE

Jesus said, "I came to give life—life in all its fullness."
JOHN 10:10 NCV

Do you ever wonder about the meaning of life? Why you're here? What it's all about? If you do, you aren't alone. Most people ponder those questions. And God is available to help you find the answers.

Inviting God into your life opens all the doors of discovery. As you get to know Him and learn to listen to His voice, you will receive insight into the reason why God created you. He will reveal His plan and purpose for your life.

Why stand around wondering, when you can have the answers to your questions? God is eager to guide you as you open the Scriptures and read about His plans and purposes. Give Him an opportunity to fill you in.

Let God have your life;
he can do more with it than you can.

DWIGHT MOODY

I will not just live my life.
I will not just spend my life.
I will invest my life.

HELEN KELLER

Life is a great big canvas;
throw all the paint on it you can.

DANNY KAYE

The value of life lies not in the length of days,
but in the use we make of them.

MICHEL DE MONTAIGNE

He that findeth his life shall lose it:
and he that loseth his life for my sake shall find it.

MATTHEW 10:39 KJV

COURAGE

Be strong and of a good courage; be not afraid, neither be thou dismayed: for the Lord thy God is with thee whithersoever thou goest.

JOSHUA 1:9 KJV

If you're a Bible reader, you've probably noticed it contains many admonitions not to fear, not to be afraid, and to be courageous. That's because this world can be one big scary place. The list of fears and phobias that plague human beings could stretch around the globe.

Fortunately, along with those admonitions, God gives the key to facing them courageously. "Don't fear, *for I am with you*," He says. When you place yourself in God's care, you are safe—not because there is no danger—but because God is bigger and more powerful than any danger you could face.

Courage is simply the ability to act in the face of fear. God will give you the courage you need as you trust Him.

Courage is fear that has said its prayers.

DOROTHY BERNARD

Courage faces fear and thereby masters it.

MARTIN LUTHER KING JR.

Fear can keep a man out of danger,
but courage can support him in it.

THOMAS FULLER

Courage consists not in blindly overlooking
danger, but in seeing and conquering it!

JEAN PAUL RICHTER

God's Spirit doesn't make cowards out of us.
The Spirit gives us power, love, and self-control.

2 TIMOTHY 1:7 CEV

GUIDANCE

*Let those who are wise listen to these proverbs
and become even wiser. And let those
who understand receive guidance.*

PROVERBS 1:5 NLT

When you were a child, someone most likely held your hand to guide you across the street or to your destination. You're no longer a child, but there is still someone who wants to help you find your way—that someone is God.

God can provide you with the guidance you need as you make your way through a complex and confusing world. He is eager to take your hand and walk with you until you reach your destination.

If you feel you are drifting, unable to get your bearings, lost or struggling, call out to God. He will help you discover where you are and where you want to go. He will instruct you through the Scriptures. And He will never leave your side.

Deep in your heart it is not guidance
that you want as much as a guide.

JOHN WHITE

I know not the way God leads me,
but well do I know my Guide.

MARTIN LUTHER

The teacher of teachers gives his guidance
noiselessly. I have never heard him speak,
and yet I know that he is within me.
At every moment he instructs me and guides me.
And whenever I am in need of it,
he enlightens me afresh.

THERESE OF LISIEUX

When we fail to wait prayerfully for God's
guidance and strength, we are saying with our
actions, if not our lips, that we do not need him.

CHARLES HUMMEL

*If I rise with the sun in the east, and settle in the west
beyond the sea, even there you would guide me.
With your right hand you would hold me.*

PSALM 139:9–10 NCV

CHURCH

*Jesus said, "I also say to you that you are Peter,
and upon this rock I will build My church;
and the gates of Hades will not overpower it."*

MATTHEW 16:18 NASB

When Jesus referred to the Church, He wasn't talking about a building. He was talking about all the people who would believe His message and gather to worship Him. He wasn't concerned with how they worshiped or where. He wasn't impressed by what they chose to wear, or what day or hour they chose to meet. He was only interested in their hearts.

You may or may not attend church regularly. Although that is important, God isn't nearly as concerned with that as He is with your relationship with Him. Do you know Him personally? Are you aware of how much He loves you and how much He wants to be part of your life? Open your heart to Him. It will soon become your favorite place of worship.

The true Church is a living organism, a body,
and believers are joined to it by
the quiet working of the Holy Spirit.

CORNELIUS STAM

The church is not wood and stone, but
the company of people who believe in Christ.

MARTIN LUTHER

We must cease to think of the church as
a gathering of institutions and organizations,
and we must get back the notion that
we are the people of God.

M. LLOYD-JONES

The church is an organism, not an organization;
a movement, not a monument.

CHARLES COLSON

God's household ... is the church of the living God,
the pillar and foundation of the truth.

1 TIMOTHY 3:15 NIV

HONESTY

You have preserved me because I was honest;
you have admitted me forever to your presence.

Psalm 41:12 TLB

Imagine a clear, still lake—so clear you can see through the water all the way to the bottom. Now see yourself taking a stick, reaching down through the water, and stirring up the muck that rests below. Before your eyes, everything changes. What was clear and still a few moments before is now cloudy and agitated.

Your heart is like that lake. As you speak, act, and live honestly, it remains clear and peaceful. But give way to deceit, color the truth, and your heart becomes muddy and agitated.

Keep the waters of your heart transparent and peaceful before God and man. Cling to the truth. Never let it out of your sight.

Honesty is the first chapter in the book of wisdom.

Thomas Jefferson

Honesty has a beautiful and refreshing simplicity about it. No ulterior motives. No hidden meanings.

CHARLES R. SWINDOLL

I consider the most enviable of all titles, the character of an honest man.

GEORGE WASHINGTON

If we be honest with ourselves, we shall be honest with each other.

GEORGE MACDONALD

An honest answer is as pleasing as a kiss on the lips.

PROVERBS 24:26 NCV

FUTURE

"I know the plans I have for you," declares the Lord,
"plans to prosper you and not to harm you,
plans to give you hope and a future."

JEREMIAH 29:11 NIV

God has promised that you will have a future—a planned path of success, a specific road to follow. You may feel you've stepped off that path and lost your way, ruining His plans for you. To God it is only a pause. His purpose and plan for your life hasn't changed.

When you feel you've taken a misstep, ask God to forgive you. He's ready and able to help you step back onto the course He's set for you. As much as you desire to move forward in life, He wants to see you succeed even more. Don't let past mistakes rob you of your future. Hope in Him and see your dreams fulfilled.

Never be afraid to trust an unknown future
to a known God.

CORRIE TEN BOOM

The only light on the future is faith.

THEODOR HOECKER

The future is God's: which means that,
wherever the individual being goes,
in life or death, God is there.

HANS KÜNG

The future is as bright as the promises of God.

ADONIRAM JUDSON

The Lord's plans will stand forever.
His ideas will last from now on.

PSALM 33:11 NCV

FELLOWSHIP

If we walk in the light, as he is in the light,
we have fellowship with one another.

1 JOHN 1:7 NIV

The Bible says God created men and women specifically for the purpose of fellowship. It is for that reason we all have a deep desire not only to have fellowship with God, but also with each other.

That doesn't mean you must have people around you all the time. It simply means that if you are a healthy, well-adjusted person, you will not shrink from interacting with others. In fact, those interactions will help you keep your bearings in the world around you, rightly perceiving your place in the whole.

Even if you don't consider yourself to be much of a people person, make an effort to reach out to someone. You'll be doing a good thing for yourself.

The virtuous soul that is alone
and without a master is like a lone burning coal;
it will grow colder rather than hotter.

JOHN OF THE CROSS

No man is an island, entire of itself;
every man is a piece of the continent,
a part of the main.

JOHN DONNE

The only basis for real fellowship with God
and man is to live out in the open with both.

ROY HESSION

Be united with other Christians.
A wall with loose bricks is not good.
The bricks must be cemented together.

CORRIE TEN BOOM

Do not be interested only in your own life,
but be interested in the lives of others.

PHILIPPIANS 2:4 NCV

GOALS

Our only goal is to please God.

2 CORINTHIANS 5:9 NCV

Goals are important. They keep you moving forward, stretching yourself, pursuing new challenges. But God doesn't want you to let your goals take over your life. He knows that if you make them too ambitious, you could find yourself lying helpless on the tracks as the train bears down on you.

Be willing to set preliminary goals—goals you are able to adjust after thoughtful consideration and prayer. And, when appropriate, the input of a trusted friend may be warranted. Always set goals that are balanced with other challenges in your life. Make them measurable and time phased. Set goals for one year at a time. Pursuing goals too far in the future can lead to fatigue and discouragement. Let God help you set goals that will work for you.

First build a proper goal. That proper goal
will make it easy, almost automatic,
to build a proper you.

GOETHE

The goal of a virtuous life is to become like God.

GREGORY OF NYSSA

You become successful the moment you start moving toward a worthwhile goal.

AUTHOR UNKNOWN

The tragedy in life doesn't lie in not reaching your goal. The tragedy lies in having no goal to reach.

BENJAMIN MAYS

Forgetting those things which are behind and reaching forward to those things which are ahead, I press toward the goal for the prize of the upward call of God in Christ Jesus.

PHILIPPIANS 3:13–14 NKJV

HELP

*Jesus said, "The Helper will teach you everything.
He will cause you to remember all the things
I told you. This Helper is the Holy Spirit whom
the Father will send in my name."*

JOHN 14:26 NCV

As the third Person of the Godhead, the Holy Spirit is eternal, omnipresent, just, good, and wise. His mission is to be your "Helper," as you go about life as a redeemed child of God.

Your Helper is constantly by your side, whispering words of encouragement in your ear, helping you find solutions to problems, comforting you during difficult times, convicting you when you are in danger of getting off track. The Holy Spirit has been called the "*paraclete*," one who walks alongside another.

It was never God's intention for you to go it alone. He knew it simply would be too difficult. Open your heart to the Holy Spirit. Let Him help you find your way.

The Holy Spirit has promised to lead us
step by step into the fullness of truth.

LEON JOSEPH SUENENS

GOD'S DAILY ANSWER
devotions to renew your soul

Call the Comforter by the term you think best—
Advocate, Helper, Paraclete, the word conveys
the indefinable blessedness of his sympathy;
an inward invisible kingdom that causes
the saint to sing through every night of sorrow.

OSWALD CHAMBERS

Jesus promised his followers that
"The Strengthener" would be with them.
This promise is no lullaby for the fainthearted.
It is a blood transfusion for courageous living.

E. PAUL HOVEY

What other help could we ever need than
that of the Holy Spirit of God?

ANDREA GARNEY

We can feel sure and say,
"I will not be afraid because the Lord is my helper."

HEBREWS 13:6 NCV

PRAYER

This is the confidence (the assurance, the privilege of
boldness) which we have in Him: [we are sure] that if
we ask anything (make any request) according to
His will (in agreement with His own plan),
He listens to and hears us.

1 JOHN 5:14 AMP

God not only created you, but He also has
redeemed you and given you instant access
to His presence through prayer. You have the
opportunity to interact with God just as you would
a loving father or a trusted friend. The Bible says
that when you speak, He will be listening.

Unfortunately, human traditions have placed
countless restrictions on the simple act of prayer.
These prescribe how, when, where, and for what
purpose prayers should be offered. While the Bible
offers models for prayer and admonitions about
attitudes in prayer, it seems that all God really expects
is you speak to Him honestly and respectfully.

Tell God what's on your mind. He's waiting to
hear from you.

Prayer is conversation with God.

CLEMENT OF ALEXANDRIA

We should speak to God from our own hearts
and talk to him as a child talks to his father.

CHARLES HADDON SPURGEON

Let your first "Good morning"
be to your Father in heaven.

KARL G. MAESER

When you can't put your prayers into words,
God hears your heart.

AUTHOR UNKNOWN

When you pray, always thank God.

COLOSSIANS 4:2 NCV

ENCOURAGEMENT

If one has the gift of encouraging others,
he should encourage.

ROMANS 12:8 NCV

The Book of Acts tells us the early Christians faced many trials and much suffering. They survived and even flourished because they received encouragement from God and each other. They took time to remind each other that they had something special, something that could never be taken from them—a living, eternal, personal relationship with Almighty God.

You, too, can receive the encouragement that comes from knowing God, and nothing you are experiencing now or will encounter in the future can take it away from you. Let God encourage your heart with words of love and promise. Then thank Him by reaching out and encouraging someone else with a kind gesture, uplifting word, or warm smile.

One of the highest of human duties is
the duty of encouragement.

WILLIAM BARCLAY

More people fail for lack of encouragement
than for any other reason.

AUTHOR UNKNOWN

Encouragement is oxygen to the soul.

GEORGE M. ADAMS

Encouragement costs you nothing to give,
but it is priceless to receive.

AUTHOR UNKNOWN

Patience and encouragement come from God.

ROMANS 15:5 NCV

PEACE

God's peace will keep your hearts and minds in
Christ Jesus. The peace that God gives is
so great that we cannot understand it.

PHILIPPIANS 4:7 NCV

Does your world sometimes get so loud you want to cover your ears? Do you find yourself frantically searching for a little peace? Relax! You don't have to look far for it, and you can take it with you wherever you go.

God's peace is like your favorite song playing over and over in your heart. It drowns out confusion, worry, anxiety, and stress. It fills you with a knowing that God has everything under control. God's peace is supernatural calm in the midst of the storm.

When you feel the world swirling around you, focus on God. Let Him turn up the music of His love in your heart until it drowns out the cares of this life.

Peace rules the day when Christ rules the mind.

AUTHOR UNKNOWN

If the basis of peace is God,
the secret of peace is trust.

J. N. FIGGIS

No God, no peace. Know God, know peace.

AUTHOR UNKNOWN

Christ alone can bring lasting peace—
peace with God—peace among men
and nations—and peace within our hearts.

BILLY GRAHAM

*You will keep him in perfect peace, whose mind is
stayed on You, because he trusts in You.*

ISAIAH 26:3 NKJV

GROWTH

Like newborn babies, crave pure spiritual milk,
so that by it you may grow up in your salvation,
now that you have tasted that the Lord is good.

1 PETER 2:2–3 NIV

Children like to measure their height to see
how much they've grown. You can measure
your spiritual growth by looking into the Scriptures.
There you will find the description of godly character
and attitudes—love, joy, peace, and patience, to
name a few. The more you grow, the more you exhibit
those characteristics in your life.

You can encourage spiritual growth in your life
by spending time with God. That might mean talking
to Him through prayer, singing His praises, or reading
the Bible—His words of instruction, encouragement,
and inspiration, written just for you.

Make sure you don't neglect your spiritual
growth. One day your body will die, but your spirit
will live on forever.

Be not afraid of growing slowly,
be afraid only of standing still.

CHINESE PROVERB

Gradual growth in grace, knowledge, faith, love,
holiness, humility, and spiritual-mindedness—
all this I see clearly taught and urged in Scripture.

J. C. RYLE

Progress in the Christian life is exactly equal to
the growing knowledge we gain of
the Triune God in personal experience.

A. W. TOZER

If we don't change, we don't grow.
If we don't grow, we are not really living.
Growth demands a temporary
surrender of security.

GAIL SHEEHY

*Grow in the grace and knowledge of our Lord
and Savior Jesus Christ.*

2 PETER 3:18 NCV

WEALTH

*Jesus said, "Your heart will always be where
your riches are."*

MATTHEW 6:21 GNT

The Bible indicates that riches can be a
mixed blessing. On the one hand, they
relieve the worry and concern about the immediacy
of personal needs, but they can also create other
problems.

The Bible says: *Give this command to those who
are rich with things of this world. Tell them not to be
proud. Tell them to hope in God, not their money. Money
cannot be trusted, but God takes care of us richly. He
gives us everything to enjoy. Tell the rich people to do
good and to be rich in doing good deeds. Tell them to be
happy to give and ready to share. By doing that, they will
be saving a treasure for themselves in heaven* (Timothy
6:17–19 NCV).

There is nothing wrong with people
possessing riches. The wrong comes when
riches possess people.

BILLY GRAHAM

The real measure of our wealth is how much
we'd be worth if we lost all our money.

JOHN HENRY JOWETT

If you want to feel rich, just count all
the things you have that money can't buy.

AUTHOR UNKNOWN

God only and not wealth, maintains the world.

MARTIN LUTHER

To enjoy your work and to accept your lot in life—
that is indeed a gift from God.

ECCLESIASTES 5:19 TLB

KINDNESS

*Clothe yourselves with compassion, kindness,
humility, gentleness and patience.*

COLOSSIANS 3:12 NIV

Do you realize that when you say a kind word or offer a kind gesture, you are imitating God? You are. The Bible says that kindness is a fruit—a by-product—of God's Holy Spirit. It is part of His character. When you treat others with kindness, you are treating them the way God treats you.

Forget the theory that too much kindness can make you appear weak or that acts of kindness should only be offered in response to kindness from others. It pleases God to see kindness flowing freely from your life, without thought of reciprocation. Rather than indicating weakness, it makes you an initiator. That takes strength and courage. So open your heart and establish kindness as part of your character.

Be the living expression of God's kindness:
kindness in your face, kindness in your eyes,
kindness in your smile, kindness in
your warm greeting.

MOTHER TERESA

A kind heart is a fountain of gladness,
making everything in its vicinity
freshen into smiles.

WASHINGTON IRVING

Constant kindness can accomplish much.
As the sun makes ice melt, kindness
causes misunderstanding, mistrust
and hostility to evaporate.

ALBERT SCHWEITZER

Be kind. Remember that everyone you meet is
fighting a hard battle.

HARRY THOMPSON

*"I am the Lord, who exercises kindness, justice
and righteousness on earth, for in these I delight,"
declares the Lord.*

JEREMIAH 9:24 NIV

THOUGHTS

Whatsoever things are true, whatsoever things are honest, whatsoever things are just, whatsoever things are pure, whatsoever things are lovely, whatsoever things are of good report; if there be any virtue, and if there be any praise, think on these things.

PHILIPPIANS 4:8 KJV

Do you sometimes feel your thoughts are carrying on a conversation without you? That probably means your mind is full of cares, worries, and negative thinking. The only way to control your thoughts is to make conscious choices concerning what you think about.

When a negative thought comes your way, try countering it by meditating on how valuable you are to God. Pause to consider His great love for you. Ponder a Bible promise. Count your blessings, recalling the times God has provided for you.

God will not usurp your power over your mind. He has given it to you, along with your free will, to order and control. But He will help you deal with your thoughts if you ask Him to.

Change your thoughts and you change your world.

NORMAN VINCENT PEALE

Our best friends and our worst enemies are o
ur thoughts. A thought can do us more good
than a doctor or a banker or a faithful friend.
It can also do us more harm than a brick.

FRANK CRANE

Keep your thoughts right, for as you think,
so are you.

HENRY H. BUCKLEY

Think positively and masterfully, with confidence
and faith, and life becomes more secure,
more fraught with action, richer in
achievement and experience.

EDDIE RICKENBACKER

*Don't copy the behavior and customs of this world,
but let God transform you into a new person by
changing the way you think.*

ROMANS 12:2 NLT

HOSPITALITY

Do not neglect to show hospitality to strangers,
for by this some have entertained angels
without knowing it.

HEBREWS 13:2 NASB

Perhaps you know someone who oozes with hospitality—someone quick to accommodate any guest, incredibly polite and cheerful, warm, considerate, cordial, and who loves to entertain. Perhaps you're a person like that—friendly and generous—or perhaps you aren't.

If you draw back from inviting people into your home, it may be time to push forward. Receiving people graciously pleases God. Just as He welcomes you into His heart and will one day invite you into His heavenly home, His desire is for you to open your heart and your home to others. Does that mean He expects you to entertain every night? Of course not. But He does expect you to do it graciously as opportunities come your way. Why not invite someone over today?

When there is room in the heart,
there is room in the house.

DANISH PROVERB

Hospitality is threefold: for one's family,
this is necessity; for strangers, this is courtesy;
for the poor, this is charity.

THOMAS FULLER

Hospitality is one form of worship.

JEWISH PROVERB

Who practices hospitality entertains
God himself.

AUTHOR UNKNOWN

*All the believers were together. ...
They broke bread in their homes and ate together
with glad and sincere hearts.*

ACTS 2:44, 46 NIV

REST

*Jesus said, "Come to Me, all you who labor
and are heavy laden, and I will give you rest."*
MATTHEW 11:28 NKJV

How was your week? Exhausting? You come home after a long week and begin the home projects that are always waiting. If you take time to rest, you may even feel a little guilty, as if you are wasting precious time or being lazy. Perish the thought.

God has actually mandated that one day of your week be set aside for rest. It will be medicine to your active mind and body. But rest shouldn't be relegated only to that day. It's also wise to take a few minutes in the course of every day to pause and take a breather.

Your Creator rested on the seventh day of creation. If Almighty God took time to rest, shouldn't you?

Take rest; a field that has rested
gives a bountiful crop.

OVID

There is no music in a rest,
but there is the making of music in it.

JOHN RUSKIN

Unless we come apart and rest a while,
we may just plain come apart.

VANCE HAVNER

How beautiful it is to do nothing
and then rest afterward.

SPANISH PROVERB

*The Lord said, "My Presence will go with you,
and I will give you rest."*

EXODUS 33:14 NKJV

FAITHFULNESS

Your faithfulness endures to all generations;
You established the earth, and it abides.

PSALM 119:90 NKJV

Faithfulness—reliability, dependability, and trustworthiness—is a characteristic so vital that other virtues lose their power without it.

Consider this: You have been volunteering for an organization that provides meals for the elderly. You have committed to be there three times a week. But suppose you have been showing up only once a week or even twice a week. Your good deed has now taken on a negative aspect. The organization and the elderly people it serves are being disadvantaged as a result of your lack of faithfulness.

God wants you to follow His example. He doesn't make promises He doesn't intend to keep. You shouldn't either. He always keeps His word. So should you.

He does most in God's great world who does his best in his own little world.

THOMAS JEFFERSON

We know that our rewards depend not
on the job itself but on the faithfulness
with which we serve God.

JOHN PAUL I

Faithfulness in little things is a big thing.

SAINT JOHN CHRYSOSTOM

God did not call us to be successful,
but to be faithful.

MOTHER TERESA

Do not let loyalty and faithfulness forsake you;
bind them around your neck,
write them on the tablet of your heart.

PROVERBS 3:3 NRSV

GOD'S LOVE

Nothing living or dead, angelic or demonic, today or tomorrow, high or low, thinkable or unthinkable—absolutely nothing can get between us and God's love.

ROMANS 8:38–39 THE MESSAGE

The very definition of love begins with God, and the very definition of God begins with love. Love is more than His character; it is the essence of His being. And the miracle, the wonder of it, is God poured out that love, poured out Himself, for you!

Before you ever breathed your first breath, spoke your first word, took your first step, He loved you. Why? Because you are His unique creation, the work of His hands. He made you in His own image, and He loves you as deeply as He loves Jesus.

Don't run from God's love—run to it! He left the decision in your hands when He gave you a free will. Now He waits for you to return His love.

Jesus did not come to make God's love possible, but to make God's love visible.

AUTHOR UNKNOWN

God's love is always supernatural,
always a miracle,
always the last thing we deserve.

ROBERT HORN

God soon turns from his wrath,
but he never turns from his love.

CHARLES HADDON SPURGEON

Every existing thing is equally upheld in
its existence by God's creative love.

SIMONE WEIL

*God's love has been poured into our hearts through
the Holy Spirit that has been given to us.*

ROMANS 5:5 NRSV

COMFORT

Whenever I am anxious and worried,
you comfort me and make me glad.

PSALM 94:19 GNT

Simple pleasures such as chocolate, a balloon bouquet, or a card may bring you a moment of comfort during a difficult time; but the comfort God gives can do so much more. It can provide a soothing balm for your nerves, free you from fear and anxiety, and fill you with hope and assurance.

Like a loving earthly father, God's heart aches to ease your pain and lift your spirit. But He will never crowd you. He'll wait patiently for the day you call on Him. Lift your face up to the heavens and ask God for His comforting touch. Let it cover you like a warm blanket and penetrate to the deepest reaches of your soul.

No affliction nor temptation, no guilt nor power of sin, no wounded spirit nor terrified conscience, should induce us to despair of help and comfort from God!

THOMAS SCOTT

In Christ the heart of the Father is revealed,
the higher comfort there cannot be than
to rest in the Father's heart.

ANDREW MURRAY

God does not comfort us to make us
comfortable, but to make us comforters.

ABRAHAM LINCOLN

It will greatly comfort you if you can see God's
hand in both your losses and your crosses.

CHARLES HADDON SPURGEON

*Now let your lovingkindness comfort me,
just as you promised.*

PSALM 119:76 TLB

HUMILITY

*Be humble and give more honor to others
than to yourselves.*

PHILIPPIANS 2:3 NCV

Exercising humility means that you are willing to waive your rights and take a lower place than might be your due. It does not require you to underrate yourself, but to live with an appropriate understanding of who you are. It is not a sign of weakness, but rather the hallmark of a healthy self-esteem.

Jesus humbled himself when He agreed to be the sacrifice for our sins. The crown Prince of heaven, the Holy Son of God allowed Himself to be beaten and crucified to pay the penalty for our sin. Because He knew exactly who He was, He could choose to humble himself on our behalf.

Embrace humility, just as Jesus did, so you might accomplish God's special mission for your life.

Humility is nothing else but a true knowledge
and awareness of oneself as one really is.

THE CLOUD OF UNKNOWING

For those who would learn God's ways,
humility is the first thing,
humility is the second, humility is the third.

SAINT AUGUSTINE OF HIPPO

If you are humble, nothing will touch you,
neither praise nor disgrace,
because you know what you are.

MOTHER TERESA

It is no great thing to be humble when you are
brought low; but to be humble when you are
praised is a great and rare attainment.

SAINT BERNARD OF CLAIRVAUX

*Be clothed with humility, for "God resists the proud,
but gives grace to the humble."*

1 PETER 5:5 NKJV

PRIORITIES

*Jesus said, Thou shalt love the Lord thy God with
all thy heart, and with all thy soul, and with all
thy mind, and with all thy strength: this is the first
commandment. And the second is like, namely this,
Thou shalt love thy neighbour as thyself.*
MARK 12:30–31 KJV

In the Bible, Jesus established a pattern for
your priorities. He said you are to first love
the Lord your God with all your heart, soul, mind,
and strength, and then your neighbor as yourself.

God is relational. He always puts others first.
And that's what He's instructed us to do in this
statement. Your relationship with God must come
first because He is the wellspring—the source—of
all you need.

God says your second priority should be yourself.
Does that surprise you? Until you are strong and
healthy, fully established in God's love, you have
little to offer anyone else.

Your last priority is to those who are nearby.
This would include your family, your friends, and of
course, the folks next door.

The main thing is to keep the main thing
the main thing!
AUTHOR UNKNOWN

When first things are put first,
second things are not suppressed but increased.

C. S. LEWIS

Tell me to what you pay attention,
and I will tell you who you are.

JOSÉ ORTEGA Y GASSET

Do not let the good things in life rob you
of the best things.

BUSTER ROTHMAN

*Jesus said, "What good will it be for a man if
he gains the whole world, yet forfeits his soul?"*

MATTHEW 16:26 NIV

COMPASSION

The Lord longs to be gracious to you, and therefore
He waits on high to have compassion on you.
ISAIAH 30:18 NASB

The Bible recounts many examples of God's kindness and compassion. He heard the cries of the Israelites as they suffered as slaves in Egypt and set them free. He responded to the grave situation of a poor widow woman by providing her with oil and meal in a time of famine. He sent His Son to redeem your life.

God doesn't change. He is just as compassionate today as He was back in Bible times. When you call out to Him, He will hear you and set in place a plan to rescue you, to comfort you, to provide for you.

God loves you. He wants to help you deal with the issues in your life. Lift your voice to Him, knowing that He will hear and pour out His compassion on you.

Man may dismiss compassion from his heart,
but God will never.

WILLIAM COWPER

One fact is clear: God did not separate himself
from human beings and their needs.
Nor did he limit his concern to
the spiritual part of man's personality.

ERWIN W. LUTZER

God's care will carry you so you can carry others.

ROBERT HAROLD SCHULLER

Man is never nearer the Divine than
in his compassionate moments.

JOSEPH H. HERTZ

As a father has compassion for his children,
so the Lord has compassion for those who fear him.

PSALM 103:13 NRSV

PATIENCE

Since God chose you to be the holy people whom
he loves, you must clothe yourselves with
tenderhearted mercy, kindness, humility,
gentleness, and patience.

COLOSSIANS 3:12 NLT

If it were not for God's patience with us, who
knows how many times He would have wiped
the slate clean and begun again. But God never gives
up. He waits and hopes and gently woos. Then He
patiently waits again for growth and maturity.

If God can find it in His heart to be patient,
shouldn't you follow His example? When you feel
frustrated and out of patience with someone—a
spouse, a friend, a coworker, a neighbor, a child, a
parent—rather than choosing to give up, hang on!
Ask God to extend your patience in supernatural
ways—to others and to yourself. Patience doesn't
make you a patsy; it makes you more like God.

Be patient with everyone,
but above all, with yourself.

SAINT FRANCIS DE SALES

He who possesses patience, possesses himself.

RAYMOND LULL

Teach us, O Lord, the disciplines of patience,
for to wait is often harder than to work.

PETER MARSHALL

Be patient toward all that is unsolved
in your heart.

DAG HAMMARSKJÖLD

Be patient when trouble comes. Pray at all times.

ROMANS 12:12 NCV

HOPE

He shall strengthen your heart,
all you who hope in the Lord.

PSALM 31:24 NKJV

Hope is a wish or desire accompanied by confident expectation of its fulfillment. You carry many hopes—earnest expectations—for your future, your family, your career, and your health. It's a mistake, though, to place your hope in people and things that will sooner or later fail you—a good job to fulfill your hope of financial prosperity, someone you hope will be a true and faithful friend. Circumstances change and people disappoint—that's life.

But God will never fail you. He is the only One who can be trusted to sustain your hope, because His power transcends circumstances and the good intentions of human beings. When you place your hope in Him, you will not be disappointed.

What oxygen is to the lungs,
such is hope for the meaning of life.

HEINRICH EMIL BRUNNER

Hope can see heaven through
the thickest clouds.

THOMAS BENTON BROOKS

Hope means faith in God
and in His omnipotence.

CARLO CARRETTO

Hope is the struggle of the soul,
breaking loose from what is perishable
and attesting her eternity.

HERMAN MELVILLE

*Put all your hope in how kind God will be
to you when Jesus Christ appears.*

1 PETER 1:13 CEV

GENTLENESS

Be gentle with one another, sensitive.
Forgive one another as quickly
and thoroughly as God in Christ forgave you.

EPHESIANS 4:32 THE MESSAGE

The Twenty-third Psalm describes God as a gentle Shepherd who cares lovingly for His sheep. Gentle Shepherd? Does that seem like an unlikely contrast to the way you perceive God—Almighty God, Mighty Warrior, Righteous Judge? But according to the Bible, gentleness is as much a part of God's character as strength and justice.

It is the gentle part of God that motivates Him to guide and sustain you through difficult times. The Creator of the universe reaches down to comfort you in times of sorrow. God does not feel gentleness compromises His strength at all—in fact, it fortifies it.

Free yourself from the idea that showing gentleness makes you appear weak. It just isn't true. God has always known that, and now you know it too.

Nothing is so strong as gentleness,
nothing so gentle as real strength.

SAINT FRANCIS DE SALES

Feelings are everywhere ... be gentle.

J. MASAI

Power can do by gentleness what
violence fails to accomplish.

LATIN PROVERB

Instead of losing, the gentle gain.
Instead of being ripped off
and taken advantage of,
they come out ahead!

CHARLES R. SWINDOLL

Let your gentleness be known to everyone.

PHILIPPIANS 4:5 NRSV

DETERMINATION

*I know whom I have believed and I am convinced
that He is able to guard what I have entrusted to
Him until that day.*

2 TIMOTHY 1:12 NASB

God never gives up! It took determination to create the Earth and all it contains. And He was determined when He created you— determined you would become all He has created you to be.

He will never bully you nor usurp the free will He has given you. But with determination, He will continue to love and care for you, waiting patiently for the day when you acknowledge His hand on your life and choose to love Him in return. He believes in you and in all you have the potential to become.

Seek Him and His wonderful plan for your life. The two of you will make a great team—united in your determination to fulfill your destiny.

A strong will, a settled purpose, an invincible determination can accomplish almost anything.

THOMAS FULLER

Lord, give me the determination
and tenacity of a weed.

Mrs. Leon R. Walters

The difference between the impossible
and the possible lies in a person's determination.

Tommy Lasorda

Be like a postage stamp—stick to one thing
until you get there.

Josh Billings

We must not become tired of doing good. …
We must not give up!

Galatians 6:9 NCV

GOODNESS

*How great is your goodness, which you have
stored up for those who fear you.*

PSALM 31:19 NIV

Goodness is a moral condition—a deliberate preference for what is right and persistence to choose and follow it. Does that sound like a standard too high for you to aspire to?

The truth is that pure goodness is an impossible dream for any human being to undertake. Fortunately, you don't have to depend on your own resources to obtain goodness. God has made a way.

First, God has wrapped you in His goodness and declared you to be "good," simply because you are His child. Then, as you spend time with Him, His goodness will literally begin to rub off on you. Slowly but surely, God will teach you to walk in His example—consistently, deliberately, persistently choosing the good and following it.

God's goodness is the root of all goodness;
and our goodness, if we have any,
springs out of his goodness

WILLIAM TYNDALE

God is all that is good, in my sight,
and the goodness that everything has is his.

JULIAN OF NORWICH

The goodness of God knows how to use our
disordered wishes and actions, often lovingly
turning them to our advantage while always
preserving the beauty of his order.

SAINT BERNARD OF CLAIRVAUX

Think of how good God is! He gives us
the physical, mental, and spiritual ability
to work in his kingdom, and then he
rewards us for doing it!

ERWIN W. LUTZER

O taste and see that the Lord is good;
happy are those who take refuge in him.

PSALM 34:8 NRSV

SUCCESS

We will shout for joy when you succeed.
We will raise a flag in the name of our God.
Psalm 20:5 NCV

Would it surprise you to know God is committed to your success? Like a loving Father, He desires to see you become all you are destined to be. He wants to help you develop your gifts, grow in character, and live a happy, fulfilled life.

God also wants to make sure you don't get caught up in misleading, temporal measures of success and miss out on those things that truly matter—the things that may seem ordinary and mundane, but in reality are the good and satisfying things in life. He wants to see you succeed in your marriage and with your children. He wants to see you sustain long, rewarding friendships and thrive in your relationship with Him.

Set your sights on becoming a success—God's way.

What a tragedy to climb the ladder of success, only to discover that the ladder was leaning against the wrong wall.

Erwin W. Lutzer

We should work to become, not to acquire.

AUTHOR UNKNOWN

Success is a journey, not a destination.

BEN SWEETLAND

It is not your business to succeed,
but to do right; when you have done so,
the rest lies with God.

C. S. LEWIS

O Lord, we beseech you, give us success!

PSALM 118:25 NRSV

GRACE

*The grace (blessing and favor) of the Lord Jesus Christ
(the Messiah) be with your spirit.*

PHILEMON 1:25 AMP

Grace is free and unmerited favor. You don't
have to do anything to receive it. When
someone performs an act of goodwill toward another
for no reason other than to show kindness, you know
grace is at work. Grace doesn't expect payment—it's
a gift given with no strings attached.

God's grace was extended to you when He
looked down from heaven and chose to make you His
child. He took upon himself the price you owed—the
price exacted by sin and your poor choices and selfish
behaviors.

Receive God's grace today. It is a gift, extended
to you without thought of reciprocation. All you
need do is reach out and take His hand. As you do,
your life will be transformed.

Grace is love that cares and stoops and rescues.

JOHN STOTT

Grace is always given to those ready
to give thanks for it.

THOMAS À KEMPIS

There is nothing but God's grace.
We walk upon it; we breathe it;
we live and die by it; it makes the nails
and axles of the universe.

ROBERT LOUIS STEVENSON

A state of mind that sees God in
everything is evidence of growth in
grace and a thankful heart.

CHARLES FINNEY

*Grace to you and peace from God our Father,
and the Lord Jesus Christ.*

ROMANS 1:7 KJV

TIME

A wise man's heart discerns both time and judgment.

ECCLESIASTES 8:5 NKJV

What if you knew exactly how much time—how many years, days, hours—you would have here on Earth? Would you make any changes in the way you live your life? It's a question worth considering.

Of course, only God knows how many days your life will contain. And although He isn't going to reveal that information to you, He has given some good advice in the Scriptures. He admonishes you to be a good steward of time, to use it wisely, sober-mindedly. And you aren't to assume that you will be here even one more day—for no one knows what lies ahead. The bottom line is, entrust yourself to God and let Him help you make every minute count.

Only eternal values can give
meaning to temporal ones.
Time must be the servant of eternity.

ERWIN W. LUTZER

Time is given us to use in view of eternity.

AUTHOR UNKNOWN

What is time? Months, years, centuries—
these are but arbitrary and outward signs,
the measure of Time, not time itself.
Time is the Life of the soul.

HENRY WADSWORTH LONGFELLOW

Time is not a commodity that can be stored for
future use. It must be invested hour by hour.

THOMAS EDISON

See then that you walk circumspectly,
not as fools but as wise, redeeming the time,
because the days are evil.

EPHESIANS 5:15–16 NKJV

CONTENTMENT

Godliness with contentment is great gain.

1 TIMOTHY 6:6 NIV

Contentment is simply being satisfied with what you have and who you are—not so easy in a world where everyone seems to be grasping for all they can get. The inner drive you feel to better yourself is God-given. It motivates you to grow in all the aspects of your life. But if that drive becomes unbalanced, it spawns insecurity and the sense that others are passing you by. If it goes unchecked, soon you will feel compelled to get ahead at all costs.

God doesn't want you always striving any more than He wants you always standing still. What He does want is for you to be satisfied—content—with who you are and what you have at any given time in your life. If you are having difficulty getting there, God can help.

A little is as much as a lot, if it is enough.

STEVE BROWN

God is most glorified in us when we are
most satisfied in him.

JOHN PIPER

The utmost we can hope for in
this life is contentment.

JOSEPH ADDISON

The secret of contentment is the realization
that life is a gift, not a right.

AUTHOR UNKNOWN

I have learned to be content with whatever I have.

PHILIPPIANS 4:11 NRSV

ANGELS

*All the angels are spirits who serve God
and are sent to help those who will receive salvation.*

HEBREWS 1:14 NCV

The Bible says angels exist and are here to care for those who will receive salvation. They are God's emissaries between heaven and Earth.

But there are some things you should understand about the ministry of angels. They are not the creatures typically described in folklore and popular art. The Bible says there are certain ways to identify an angel sent from God.

First, God's angels don't draw attention to themselves. Glorifying God and carrying out His instructions are an angel's only concerns. In addition, the actions of God's angels never contradict the Holy Scriptures or move contrary to God's character.

Thank God for the angels that move invisibly in and out of your life. One day, you might even spot one doing God's bidding.

Millions of spiritual creatures walk the earth unseen, both when we sleep and when we awake.

JOHN MILTON

An angel is a spiritual being created by
God without a body, for the service of
Christendom and the Church.

MARTIN LUTHER

An angel's function is to execute the plan of
divine providence even in earthly things.

SAINT THOMAS AQUINAS

In Scripture we uniformly read that angels are
heavenly spirits, whose obedience
and ministry God employs.

JOHN CALVIN

God has put his angels in charge of you.
They will watch over you wherever you go.

PSALM 91:11 NCV

GENEROSITY

A generous person will be enriched.

Proverbs 11:25 NRSV

Have you ever given any thought to what the world would be like if God were a tight-fisted miser? It's impossible to imagine the mountains without snow-capped peaks, trees without branches full of blossoms, children without innocence and laughter, life without redemption. God has been indescribably generous with us, and all He asks in return is that we follow His example by being generous with one another.

The next time you reach out to help someone, make it a generous offering—more than is required, more than would be expected. Instead of giving only what you no longer want or need, give of your best, your finest. Open your arms and your heart, and give generously—like God.

He who gives what he would as readily throw away, gives without generosity; for the essence of generosity is in self-sacrifice.

Sir Henry Taylor

The truly generous is the truly wise,
and he who loves not others, lives unblest.

Henry Home

You do not have to be rich to be generous.
If he has the spirit of true generosity,
a pauper can give like a prince.

Corrine U. Wells.

The test of generosity is not how much you give,
but how much you have left.

Author Unknown

*"Bring the whole tithe into the storehouse, t
hat there may be food in my house. Test me in this,"
says the Lord Almighty, "and see if I will not throw
open the floodgates of heaven and pour out so much
blessing that you will not have room enough for it."*

Malachi 3:10 niv

PROVISION

My God shall supply all your need according to
His riches in glory by Christ Jesus.

PHILIPPIANS 4:19 NKJV

The Bible says God has made a firm commitment to provide for those who place themselves in His care. That doesn't mean He's passing out free lunches. He still expects us to work diligently and responsibly so we will have enough for ourselves and even some left over to share with others.

In every life, however, there are times of need. That need could be financial, but it could just as easily be emotional, physical, or even spiritual. No matter what it is you lack, God is faithful and He will provide what you need.

The next time you find yourself deficient in an area, don't try to go it alone. Call on God and expect to see His provision.

Where God guides, He provides.

AUTHOR UNKNOWN

He who gives us teeth will give us bread.

JEWISH PROVERB

The Lord my pasture shall prepare,
and feed me with a shepherd's care;
His presence shall my wants supply,
and guard me with a watchful eye.

JOSEPH ADDISON

Get the spindle ready
and God will send the flax.

AUTHOR UNKNOWN

God has shown kindness by giving you rain from
heaven and crops in their seasons;
he provides you with plenty of food
and fills your hearts with joy.

ACTS 14:17 NIV

STRENGTH

The Lord is the strength of my life.

PSALM 27:1 NKJV

Can you remember a time when you felt so weak, so exhausted that you were sure you couldn't go on? Perhaps it was the result of a physical illness, the death of a loved one, or a time of extraordinary mental stress.

You should know that in those difficult times, God has promised to undergird you with His divine strength. That provision is available to you whenever you need it. All you have to do is ask.

You don't have to wait until you're heart becomes overwhelmed to call on Him. He is waiting to hold you up and fill you with inner strength— during bad times and even during good times. Just call on Him!

The weaker we feel, the harder we lean on God. And the harder we lean, the stronger we grow.

JONI EARECKSON TADA

The Lord doesn't promise to give us something
to take so we can handle our weary moments. He
promises us himself. That is all.
And that is enough.

CHARLES R. SWINDOLL

When a man has no strength,
if he leans on God, he becomes powerful.

DWIGHT LYMAN MOODY

When God is our strength,
it is strength indeed; when our strength
is our own, it is only weakness.

SAINT AUGUSTINE OF HIPPO

On the day I called, You answered me;
You made me bold with strength in my soul.

PSALM 138:3 NASB

PRAISE

Shout to the Lord, all the earth;
break out in praise and sing for joy!

PSALM 98:4 NLT

Birds sing, tree branches dance in the wind, and God gave you a voice to sing praise to Him. Maybe you don't feel your voice warrants a microphone and stage, but to God's ears, there is no lovelier sound. It ushers you into His presence.

Your praise doesn't need to be limited to singing either. Shout to the Lord with thanksgiving. Praise Him for the wondrous works of His hands in your life. Dance and jump and clap and, on occasion, sit quietly and worshipfully in His presence.

God is eager to receive your praise, no matter how you choose to give it. Like a loving father glowing in the warmth of his children's adulations, God cherishes the praises of His children.

There is nothing that pleases God
so much as praise.

AUTHOR UNKNOWN

Man's chief work is the praise of God.

SAINT AUGUSTINE OF HIPPO

If any one would tell you the shortest,
surest way to all happiness and all perfection,
he must tell you to make it a rule to yourself
to thank and praise God for everything
that happens to you.

WILLIAM LAW

Praising God is one of the highest
and purest acts of religion. In prayer we act
like men; in praise we act like angels.

THOMAS WATSON

I will praise You, O Lord, with my whole heart; …
I will sing praise to Your name, O Most High.

PSALM 9:1–2 NKJV

TOPICAL INDEX

Additional copies of this book and other titles from ELM HILL BOOKS are available from your local bookstore.

Other titles in this series:

God's Daily Answer for Teachers
God's Daily Answer for Women